BOSTON
PUBLIC
LIBRARY

FIORELLO
HIS HONOR, THE LITTLE FLOWER

written and

Atheneum · 1981 · New York

FIORELLO
HIS HONOR, THE LITTLE FLOWER
Illustrated by GLORIA KAMEN

*for ELLIOT, whose patience, love and support
never seem to run out*

The Dick Tracy comic strip is reprinted by permission of
the Chicago Tribune-New York News Syndicate, Inc.

Library of Congress Cataloging in Publication Data

Kamen, Gloria.   Fiorello.

  SUMMARY: A biography of Fiorello La Guardia who
started his political career in the House of Representatives
before gaining national fame as the mayor
of New York City from 1934 to 1945.

  1. La Guardia, Fiorello Henry, 1882-1947—Juvenile
literature. 2. New York (N.Y.)—Politics and
government—1898-1951—Juvenile literature.
3. New York (N.Y.)—Mayors—Biography—Juvenile
literature. 4. Legislators— United States—Biography—
Juvenile literature. 5. United States.
Congress. House—Biography—Juvenile literature.
[1. La Guardia, Fiorello Henry, 1882-1947.
2. Mayors] I. Title.
F128.5.L18K35   974.7′104′0924   [B]   [92]   81-2282
ISBN 0-689-30869-8   AACR2

Text and pictures copyright © 1981 by Gloria Kamen
All rights reserved
Published simultaneously in Canada by
McClelland & Stewart, Ltd.
Manufactured by The American Book/Stratford Press,
Saddle Brook, New Jersey
First Edition

CONTENTS

	Introduction	3
1.	East to West	7
2.	Papa Achille Goes to War	15
3.	Napoleon and the Little Lawyer	23
4.	Fiorello Goes to Congress	31
5.	The Little Flower of New York City	37
6.	The Funnies and Fiorello	45
7.	Goodby, Little Flower	53
	Epilogue	59

Almost no one remembers who was the first mayor of New York* (his name was Thomas Willett) or the names of most of the ninety-eight others who came before Fiorello Henry LaGuardia, The Little Flower.

This is the story of why this lively, hard-working man is still loved and remembered long after his twelve years as Mayor.

* *Peter Stuyvesant was governor of New Amsterdam, not a mayor.*

A fire truck, siren blaring, went racing through the crowded streets of Manhattan. A long, black limousine chased behind. The fire chief, also on his way to the three-alarm fire, recognized the limousine. The Mayor was going to still another city fire. Last time, they treated the Mayor for frostbitten cheeks because he stayed out in the freezing cold too long. Another time he came out of a smoldering building covered with soot from head to toe. The firemen only recognized him because of his round figure and black Stetson cowboy hat.

Each day the Mayor, Fiorello Henry La Guardia, went to work in his cowboy hat, his papers stuffed into an old leather briefcase. He was very short, only five feet two inches. The hat made him look a little taller. It also reminded him of Arizona, where he grew up.

1.
EAST TO WEST

But Arizona was not where Fiorello was born. He was born in a house on Sullivan Street in New York City. His father, Achille Luigi La Guardia, and his mother, Irene, came to the United States from Italy, so it was natural for them to give their children Italian names: Gemma for their daughter, and Fiorello for their new son. It was Mama Irene who named Fiorello after his grandmother, Fiorina. The name means "little flower" in Italian.

Grandma Fiorina Coen came from a well-known Jewish family who had lived in Trieste for over three hundred years. One of them had been a prime minister.

When Irene Coen and Achille La Guardia married, they left Italy on their wedding day and sailed to America. Achille was a musician. He was a slim and handsome man with a wide moustache and dark beard. In his bandmaster uniform, he looked like an Italian duke. Mama Irene was small, with

beautiful dark eyes. Fiorello looked like his mother: short, round and dark-eyed.

When Fiorello was three years old, Achille Luigi took a job as bandmaster for the U. S. Army's Eleventh Infantry. The family moved from army post to army post, from New York to the Dakotas. At age nine, Fiorello and his family moved to Fort Whipple in Arizona Territory. Arizona, a vast, empty area except for some wildlife and a few Indian tribes, was not yet a state. The army, local sheriffs and an occasional town mayor tried to keep order in the lands of the far West. Fort Whipple was built to protect

farmers and gold prospectors from the Apache Indians who were angered by mining and farming right in the middle of the Apache hunting grounds. The Apaches tried to drive away the prospectors; the army tried to drive away the Apaches.

Gemma and Fiorello went to school in Prescott, one-and-a-half miles from their adobe house on the fort. Prescott had one school, three breweries, twenty saloons, and a drugstore. Stores had false wooden fronts and Roth's Drugstore sold newspapers that were already a week old. This didn't matter to the people of Prescott. The rest of the world seemed to be very far away from the town surrounded by miles of empty desert and high mountains. It didn't matter a bit to Fiorello that his favorite comic strip, "The Yellow Kid," took a week to get to Prescott . . . so long as it arrived. Comic strips were new to American newspapers and Fiorello became a fan.

Gemma, just a bit older than her brother, went to school each day to see her friends, do her schoolwork and to get good grades. Fiorello went knowing he would get into a fight. He got into a fight in the schoolyard daily.

"I licked him every day," said Joe Bauer, his classmate. "Every day, because Fiorello came back for more."

"The Little Flower," Fiorello, was tough. In no way did he resemble a tender blossom. He was, in fact, more like the round, prickly cactus that grew around Fort Whipple. And like the cactus, had to be handled with care.

In one of his fights in the schoolyard, Fiorello was swinging with both fists at a boy much taller than himself. His punches weren't landing. His anger grew. Suddenly he stopped the fight, ran into the classroom and dragged out a chair. Climbing onto the chair, Fiorello continued the fight, throwing

punches with both fists. He didn't win the fight . . . but neither did the other boy.

It wasn't only fights that caused Fiorello trouble. It seemed he was a headache to his teachers in other ways. He often returned from school with the marks of a whack across his legs from the teacher's ruler. It seems that sticking closely to the rules was not part of his nature . . . and never would be.

During his lunch hour, he often raced to the courthouse near school to listen to Mayor Bucky O'Neill argue a case. There was always lots of excitement at the courthouse and Fiorello could repeat what he heard there more easily than he could repeat his lessons.

"Ah, Fiorello," his mother would say. "If you only knew your schoolwork as well as you know what those politicians say. . . ."

Frontier life at Fort Whipple suited Fiorello. He liked the bugle calls, the drills, the call-to-arms and the parades. He made friends with the soldiers, who taught him how to ride wild broncos and how to shoot. He went camping in the hills with them. Papa Achille taught Fiorello how to play the banjo and the cornet. Sister Gemma learned to play the violin. A younger brother, Richard, played the piano. Papa Achille secretly hoped that some day Fiorello would become another John Philip Sousa. Sousa, the man who wrote the patriotic marches played by the army band, was loved and admired by Achille.

But hard as he tried, Fiorello never managed to become a great musician, composer, prizefighter, or jockey. At age fourteen, he wanted to be all of these and more.

2.

PAPA ACHILLE GOES TO WAR

A year later, in 1898, the United States went to war with Spain. Achille was sent to fight even though he was more musician than he was a soldier. Fiorello wanted to be with his father and tried to enlist in the army. The army wouldn't have him. Fifteen-year-old Fiorello was told he was too young, too short, and too light in weight. What they had not noticed was his confidence . . . and optimism.

He looked for some other way to be sent to Mobile, Alabama, where his father was stationed. Charging into the newspaper office of *The St. Louis Post-Dispatch,* his four feet eleven inches brimming with enthusiasm, Fiorello asked for a job. The editor of the *Post-Dispatch,* unlike the army, noticed his confidence more than his lack of size. He was given a job as a reporter without pay and sent to Mobile. Perhaps the editor also remembered a story and photo that appeared in a recent issue of the *Dispatch.* The story told of a fire in Jefferson Barracks

and how a brave young fellow raced into the burning building, grabbed his cornet and blew the fire call. The cornetist, it turned out, was Fiorello. It was the first and last time Fiorello was praised in the newspapers for playing the cornet. But it wasn't the last time he was in the papers for blowing his own horn!

When the Spanish-American War ended, Achille La Guardia, weak and in poor health, was discharged from the army. He had had food poisoning from canned meat, or as the soldiers called it, "embalmed beef." Along with malaria, food poisoning had killed more soldiers than all the battles fought in the war. Achille received a medical discharge and an eight-dollar-a-month pension. He took his family to New York and later to Trieste, in Europe, where he died. Fiorello went to work to help support his mother, sister and younger brother.

In the nearby city of Fiume, he found a job working for the United States government. Fiume, a port city in Austria-Hungary (which is now in Yugoslavia), was filled with people who spoke many different languages. Fiorello soon learned to speak Italian and Croatian (two of the languages spoken in Fiume) almost as well as he could speak English. After several years, when it seemed he could not get ahead in his job, he decided to return to America to study law.

He had very little money. In order to save the boat fare, he applied for a job as translator on a British ship leaving Fiume for America. The captain needed someone to translate the Italian and Croatian languages of his passengers into English. When he was not busy translating, Fiorello helped the ship's doctor vaccinate the one thousand eight hundred immigrants on board against smallpox.

The immigrants, unlike tourists and travelers, came to start a new life in America. Whole families, from infants to grandparents, left their towns, villages and cities carrying all they owned in a few lumpy bundles or wicker baskets. Many of them left from the city of Fiume every month for New York City, the gateway to the "New World." But when the ships arrived in America, they docked at a tiny island in New York Harbor, Ellis Island. There, each new immigrant was checked, examined and given official papers to enter the United States. For some who were found to be sick, the "gate" was never

opened. They were returned on the very next ship to the country they had just left. It made Fiorello sad and angry to see this happen over and over again. It was so easy to prevent. Why not examine all immigrants in Europe *before* they cross the Atlantic Fiorello asked. But the United States Government was not used to taking advice from a twenty-two-year-old employee.

Fiorello, not an immigrant, was returning to his native land and to the city where he was born. Like the immigrants, he was coming to stay.

3.

NAPOLEON AND THE LITTLE LAWYER

Now a young man of twenty-three, Fiorello wanted to do what he could to help the many poor people who came to America to find a better life. Often what they found was more poverty. Many did not speak English and were confused by the laws and customs of the new country. They needed help to fight for better jobs, better pay and better housing. Fiorello's ability to speak several languages made it very easy for him to find a job at Ellis Island where he worked with the thousands of new immigrants arriving each month. Each morning he took the ferry from Manhattan to Ellis Island where he helped the newcomers, the Vladmirs, the Krystofs, and Enricos, deal with forms and questions they didn't understand. Each evening he returned by ferry to his classes at New York University Law School, barely managing to stay awake until class ended.

After finishing law school, Fiorello opened a law office in a poor section of the city. His waiting room was quickly filled with people seeking help. They were mostly poor. They came because his fees were very low. They ranged, in fact, from very little to nothing at all! He was almost as poor as his clients . . . but not in ambition. On his desk was a small statue of Napoleon. Napoleon was General of all the French armies when he was only twenty-eight years old. Fiorello was twenty-eight.

Fiorello Henry La Guardia decided to go into politics and run for public office.

He joined the local Republican Club. The Democratic Party was running New York City and doing a terrible job of it. Fiorello's ambition was to fight, not join "Tammany Hall," the name given those Democrats who controlled New York.

New Yorkers began to notice the lively little lawyer who made speeches on street corners, in labor halls and anywhere else people would listen. In his high, sometimes squeaky voice, he explained, argued, or joked in Italian, English or Yiddish, depending on his audience. Sometimes it was a blend of languages. Sometimes he was called in to settle fights between Italian and Jewish factory workers. Other times he walked the picket lines daring the police to arrest him. They didn't.

Fiorello then decided to run for the United States Congress. As a Congressman, he felt he could do so much more to improve the life of the city's poor. It also meant a challenge . . . a big one. Nothing suited Fiorello better.

His chance came in 1914 when he was thirty-two years old.

Petitions were being filled out for a Republican candidate for Congress. Democrats always won the

election in the 25th Assembly District. This was the district where Fiorello lived and from which he would need to be elected. No Republican had ever won in his district, so it was understood that anyone running on the Republican ticket would lose. Still, the Republicans had to find someone.

"Who wants to run for Congress?" asked Clarence Fay, leader of the District.

"I do!" La Guardia said eagerly.

"Okay, put La Guardia down," said Fay.

"Hey, La Guardia, what's your first name?"

"Fiorello," he said.

Fay looked up. "Fiorello?" He was stunned.

"Let's get someone whose name we can spell," said Fay.

Fiorello was not put off. If they didn't know his name now, they were certainly going to by the end of his campaign.

He spelled his name slowly.

"F . . . I . . . O . . . R . . . E . . . L . . . L . . . O."
And Fay wrote it down.

When the official list was printed, his name came out as FLOULLO.

Making speeches came naturally to Fiorello. He had been doing it since he was a boy. Then, he had only Gemma as his audience . . . and Gemma did not always enjoy having this special privilege.

But in the area of the 25th Assembly District, the colorful, easy style of Fiorello's talks began to attract crowds. Even his Democratic opponent was impressed by his energetic campaign.

Even so, he lost his first election.

When the election campaign came up again two years later, Fiorello was ready to try again. Round and compact as a basketball, with almost as much bounce, Fiorello traveled around the district making speeches on street corners, in tenements and in union halls. He plastered his old Ford with huge signs and drove around the city giving out handbills with a smiling picture of himself.

This time he won the election . . . much to the surprise of almost everyone but Fiorello.

Winning the election made him one of the youngest men in Congress and the first Italian-American in the House of Representatives in the history of the United States. He was thirty-four.

In Congress, they spelled his name correctly.

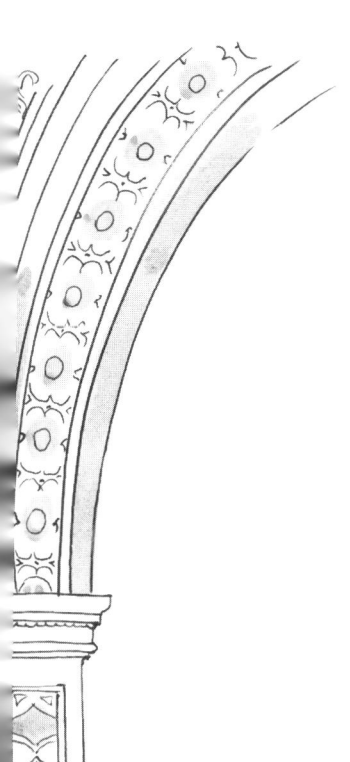

4.

FIORELLO GOES TO CONGRESS

Fiorello went to live in Washington, D.C. It was as a young congressman that he first started wearing his large cowboy hat.

War broke out in Europe in 1914 and the United States entered the war three years later. Thirty-four-year-old Congressman La Guardia left Congress to join the brand new American Air Force. Several years earlier, he had learned to fly in a school on Long Island run by an Italian friend, Bellanca. In exchange, Fiorello taught his friend how to drive a car.

Trading his cowboy hat for the goggles and leather cap of a fighter pilot, Fiorello left Washington, D.C. to join an American fighter squadron in Foggia, Italy. His style of flying was similar to his way of riding wild broncos . . . grab the saddle horn and hang on. It soon earned him the name "Flying Devil."

In 1918, the war ended and Fiorello had survived both the war and his own flying. He returned to the United States decorated with an Italian medal and the gold leaf of a major in the Air Force. Trading back his leather cap for his black Stetson, he returned to politics once more. With only a week left in which to campaign for his seat in Congress, Fiorello was voted back for a second term. He moved back to Washington, D.C. with his young bride, Thea, the beautiful girl he had fallen in love with before the war.

He met Thea, a young dress designer from Trieste (his mother's native city), during a garment workers' strike. He fell in love with her frail beauty. She admired and shared his idealism.

The marriage lasted just three short years. Thea, only twenty-five years old, died of tuberculosis, the dread disease of the big cities. Lack of fresh air and long work days often helped bring on the deadly lung infection.

Depressed and brokenhearted, Fiorello returned to his work in Congress. It was many years before he decided to remarry, and when he did, he

chose the one woman who knew him best, who could put up with his temper, his work habits and his ambition. She had been doing it for twelve years as his secretary and campaign manager. Her name was Marie Fischer. He jokingly said later that he fired a good secretary only to get a terrible cook. Marie knew better than to take this seriously. They had a happy marriage.

Confident and optimistic again, Fiorello returned to his work in Congress. His fiery speeches in favor of a shorter work week, unemployment insurance, and old-age pensions made him unpopular with many of his fellow Congressmen but a hero to the poor people of this country. Until the Norris-La Guardia Act became a law, which he and Senator Norris wrote and sponsored, any worker who joined a union or went on strike could lose his job or end up in jail.

5.

THE LITTLE FLOWER OF NEW YORK CITY

In the years from 1922 to 1932, the United States and most of Europe slid from prosperity into a deep economic depression. The city of New York was no different. It was suffering the effects of four years of mass unemployment, crooked politics and bad management. Almost a third of the people who needed to work were out of a job. A former Tammany mayor of New York, "Gentleman Jimmy Walker," as he was called, spent more money on his clothes than the city spent on milk for schoolchildren. (Mayor O'Brien, who succeeded Walker, wasn't much better.) Friends and supporters of La Guardia urged him to leave Congress and run for mayor. He agreed.

Fiorello fought hard to be elected. He wanted very much to be Mayor of New York City. Just as much, he wanted to see the corrupt Tammany giant defeated for good.

Tammany Chiefs

When it seemed on election night that Fiorello would win, Tammany Democrats tried to steal the victory. They planned to stuff the 400 voting machines that had not yet been counted with fake votes for their candidate.

The "little giant killer" was ready for just this kind of trick. La Guardia ordered 400 patrol cars to collect the voting machines, "As fast as God will let you!" When the machines were opened and the votes counted, he became the ninety-ninth Mayor of New York City.

Fiorello's first day as Mayor began at midnight on January 1, 1933. It started with a bang, like a twenty-one-gun salute! After being sworn in by Judge Seabury, he picked up the telephone and called his Police Commissioner and ordered him to arrest the most notorious gangster in the city, "Lucky Luciano." Luciano was later convicted and forced to leave the country. Word soon spread to all the racketeers and "tinhorns" that it was going to be tough to earn a dishonest living in New York. "Tinhorn" was the name used for dishonest gamblers when Fiorello was a boy.

Behind the huge oak desk in the Mayor's office, Fiorello was faced with all the problems of feeding, housing, protecting and educating a city of seven-and-a-half million people. New York, divided into five boroughs, had more people than the populations of Philadelphia, Detroit, and Los Angeles added together. Mayor La Guardia felt sure honest,

hard work would cure the city's troubles. But sometimes it seemed Napoleon's job of running the French army was far easier than running the city of New York!

Pictures and stories of "His Honor, The Little Flower," as the newspapers liked to call La Guardia, appeared regularly. They showed him behind his desk, shirt collar open, sleeves rolled up, pointing a finger at a group of glum-faced commissioners ... or mopping his brow after an argument with a deputy. The Mayor's hot temper was famous. Sometimes it seemed to rock and shake City Hall like a pot boiling over. The Mayor, in a happier mood, was photographed leading a symphony orchestra or marching in front of a parade on Fifth Avenue. When not at his desk at City Hall, he traveled the five boroughs visiting schools, hospitals, police stations and city agencies.

At times he visited the markets where food was brought into the city. Very early in the morning when the fishing boats docked on the Hudson River, the Mayor's car drove to the Fulton Fish Market. With his favorite cigar jiggling from the corner of his mouth, the Mayor strode between the bins, poking his finger into the side of a wet fish. Satisfied that the fish was fresh, he then checked the price. If the price seemed low enough, he wrote it on a slip of paper —not as a note to his wife—it was to remind him to recommend fish to the other two or three million shoppers in the city.

WNYC is a radio station owned by New York City and every Sunday afternoon at one o'clock, the Mayor spoke over the radio from his desk at City Hall.

"Fish, buy fish," the Mayor would say earnestly to his thousands of listeners. He recommended fish so often that some New Yorkers gave him the nick-

name, "The Little Flounder."

"But go slow on buying those snapbeans until next week . . . Oranges! Yes, I'm going to talk to you about oranges again."

And in more confiding tones, the Mayor would tell shoppers to buy oranges by the pound instead of by the dozen. It was cheaper that way, he said.

Mayor La Guardia's program, called "Talk to the People," was popular for the same reason his campaign speeches always collected an audience . . . no one knew what he would say next. Sometimes he even gave messages to his wife on the air, upsetting the program manager, Mr. Novik.

Mr. Novik had to remind the Mayor that personal messages on the radio were against government regulations. Mr. Novik was always a bit nervous when the Mayor spoke on WNYC.

DICK TRACY

6.

THE FUNNIES AND FIORELLO

Near the end of his third term as mayor, Fiorello made his most famous "Talk to the People." It was during the newspaper strike of July, 1945. Newspaper delivery men had walked off their jobs on Saturday night. The Sunday papers were not delivered.

Sunday, as usual, the Mayor drove to his office before noon. The corridors of City Hall were already filled with tourists, commissioners and officials waiting to hear the Mayor's talk.

It was a hot July morning. Shortly after twelve noon, Fiorello dropped into his black swivel chair, perspiration trickling down his cheeks. He went through his scribbled notes. At 12:55 p.m. the Mayor shoved the papers on his desk to one side and reached for the microphone, his black hair falling over his forehead.

He started his talk as usual with tips on food—this time, cabbage—how to cook it and why it is

good for you. Then he said, "If you have any children, bring them around the radio in thirty seconds. I have a message for them." With barely a pause, he said he knew children were disappointed because they did not get the "funnies" (his name for the comic strips in the newspapers).

With the Sunday comic section of the *Daily News* spread out on his desk, Fiorello turned to "Dick Tracy" and started to read:

"Ahhhh . . . what do we have here? The gardener.

"Stabbed! Bleeding . . . all over the floor! . . . Blood. . . ."

Then he talked to his audience in a hushed tone about Dick Tracy, the tireless detective, Dick Tracy, always slim—not like Commissioner Valentine's detectives. They had a way of getting *fat*. (Commissioner Valentine was head of the city's police force.)

"Now get this picture," continued the Mayor.

" 'Breathless' (the girl Dick Tracy is trying to capture) has hidden herself in a laundry truck . . . along with a pot of money. Money! Fifty thousand dollars . . . in a pot. Now the truck stops for a traffic light . . . (You should always stop, children," confided the Mayor, "when the light is red.) Oh, the money . . . all that money . . . is spilling out of the pot! And now we see Dick Tracy, with his fine chiseled profile, talking to the dignified Mrs. Van Hoosen. What's this? That laundry truck driver. Yes, he's found Breathless! And what does he say? He says, 'Well, mangle my shorts and call me rough-dry! I've never picked up a bag like this before!' "

The Mayor finished reading and folded the comics. He wiped his brow and glanced at Mr. Novik. "We will find out what happens tomorrow, and we will let you know in case you cannot get the papers at home."

The audience in the mayor's office applauded loud and long. Mr. Novik didn't see what was so special about the funnies. He never read them himself. He wondered who was going to be given the job of reading the funnies tomorrow as the Mayor promised. He hoped the newspaper strike would end soon. Many of the nearly two million listeners —old and young—disagreed. They were almost willing to put up with the strike if the Mayor would continue reading the funnies to them on Sunday.

But the Mayor did more than entertain the people of New York. His exaggerated behavior often had a serious purpose, as in the incident at a New Jersey airport.

On a flight from Chicago to New York City the TWA plane in which Mayor La Guardia was a passenger landed at Newark Airport. All commercial flights landed across the Hudson River because New York City still lacked an airport big enough for them.

The little Mayor refused to leave the plane—his ticket read "New York" and the plane had not landed in New York! After endless arguing with Fiorello sitting stubbornly glued to his chair, the pilot decided to fly the nearly empty plane to a small air field across the river in Brooklyn. A story about the flight to Brooklyn was in all the newspapers the next day.

He had made his point. New York City needed its own large airport. After years of complaining, pushing, and demanding, an airport, bearing his name, was finally built.

7.

GOODBY, LITTLE FLOWER

For twelve busy years, Fiorello La Guardia used his temper, brains, driving energy and wit to make New York a better city, especially for those he cared most about—the children, and the honest, hard-working citizens. During his first six months as Mayor, 400 new playgrounds were built. He put the unemployed to work planting sixty-six thousand trees and a million new shrubs in parks all over the city. New bridges, tunnels, highways, and housing provided work for as many as forty-five thousand people. Racketeers were sent to jail or left New York for safer areas (across the Hudson River). The city was being cleaned up in more ways than one!

In 1945, Fiorello La Guardia was finishing his third term as Mayor at the same time the United States came to the end of the Second World War. He decided not to seek a fourth term. Tall, good-looking William O'Dwyer was elected the new Mayor. Shaking hands in the office at City Hall, Fior-

ello La Guardia wished him good luck.

"Now," he said to O'Dwyer, "you'll have a permanent headache."

Before stepping into his Ford sedan, Fiorello took off his big black hat and waved good-bye to the reporters, photographers and friends standing outside City Hall.

As the car drove toward his apartment through the narrow streets of lower Manhattan, an airplane looped and turned above the New York skyline. In puffs of smoke, it spelled up the word, "GOOD-YEAR" over and over across the clear afternoon sky. The skywriter was advertising a brand of automobile tires. It could have been a tribute to the departing Mayor.

He had given the city twelve good years.

La Guardia went on giving advice to the people of New York on two radio programs, in newspapers and in magazines. Then when the Second World War ended President Harry S Truman made him Director of United Nations Relief (UNRRA) for all of Europe and Asia. He had to find ways to "feed, clothe and give material hope to several *hundred million* human beings who were victims of the war."

One of the war victims he helped was his own sister, Gemma, who had survived a Nazi concentration camp.

True to his unshakable rule that he would give no favors or rewards to friends or family, Gemma had to wait her turn (almost one-and-a-half years) before she could enter the U.S. Of course, he made sure that she was well cared for in the meantime.

Fiorello's health began to fail in 1946 and he was forced to give up his job with UNRRA. He died in 1947, mourned by the city that loved him and that he loved so much.

BIBLIOGRAPHY

Cuneo, Ernest. *Life with Fiorello,* Macmillan, 1955.
Gluck, Gemma La Guardia. *My Story,* McKay, 1961.
Heckscher, August. *When La Guardia Was Mayor, New York's Legendary Years,* Norton, 1978.
La Guardia, Fiorello. *The Making of an Insurgent, 1882-1919,* Lippincott, 1959.
Mann, Arthur. *La Guardia, A Fighter Against His Times,* Lippincott, 1948.
--------. *La Guardia Comes to Power—1933,* Lippincott, 1965.
Manners, William. *Patience and Fortitude: Fiorello La Guardia,* Harcourt, 1976.
Moses, Robert. *La Guardia—A Salute and a Memoir,* Simon & Schuster, 1957.
Rodman, Bella. *Fiorello La Guardia.* Hill & Wang, 1962.

My thanks also to the following for use of their materials:

The New York Historical Society
The Library of Congress Print Collection
The New York Public Library
The New York Daily News
The Museum of the City of New York